SOUTH-WEST ENGLAND FROM ABOVE

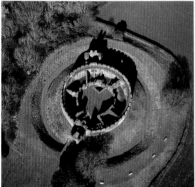

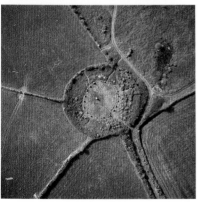

INTRODUCTION

IN THE SOUTH-WEST OF ENGLAND, the sea is never far away. The region consists of a long peninsula of three counties, Somerset, Devon and Cornwall, each of them steeped in history and legend, of which King Arthur is but one. Here is the southernmost point of England, rolling moorlands, low-lying fen and marshland, spectacular limestone caves and gorges. There are islands, too. The beautiful Scilly Isles off the south-western tip of Cornwall are famed for their mild climate; while Lundy Island, off the northern coast of Devon, is rugged and remote. The climate of the south-west benefits from the warm Atlantic gulf stream, bringing mild, though rather wet weather, all year round. Palm trees and subtropical plants that can survive the winter adorn resorts and private gardens. Holidaymakers flock here to enjoy sandy beaches, rocky coves and quaint fishing villages. Artists and writers come here for inspiration. Local family names can be traced back for centuries. This is indeed a special part of England.

Somerset is bordered on the north by the great estuary of the Severn, and on the south by the English Channel as it widens out to meet the Atlantic. This county is rich in pasture, and Saxon farmers brought their cattle to graze here over 1,300 years ago. If the north coast of Devon is abrupt and dramatic, with high cliffs rising from the Atlantic surf, the south coast is luxuriant and colourful, with a patchwork of fields reaching down to the coast in between the many resort towns and villages. Inland are networks of narrow lanes, winding, climbing and descending steep hills and valleys. Cornwall has an untamed windswept feel to it, with rugged hills, valleys and fields bounded by pale stone walls. Streams rush down to meet the sea in lonely rocky coves, while close by are picturesque fishing villages.

Twelve thousand years ago, Stone Age peoples inhabited caves in the Mendips in Somerset, hunting woolly rhinoceros and other large mammals. Later, Bronze Age peoples constructed timber tracks to cross the Somerset Levels and built stone houses in Cornwall. Stone circles and burial barrows still litter the landscape. The Celts fortified hill after hill in Somerset with massive earthworks to protect their tiny communities from raiders. They were unable to hold out against the Romans however, who left their mark in straight roads, mines, and the famous hot baths of Bath. Castles, abbeys, and lonely church towers are constant reminders of a rich and fascinating past. Everywhere, settlers of long ago have left their traces on the landscape, some of which are best seen from the air.

Photographs from top to bottom: Glastonbury Tor, Restormel Castle, Exeter Cathedral, Boscawen-un Stone Circle

PHOTOGRAPHS, TEXT AND DESIGN BY ADRIAN WARREN AND DAE SASITORN

MYRIAD BOOKS LIMITED

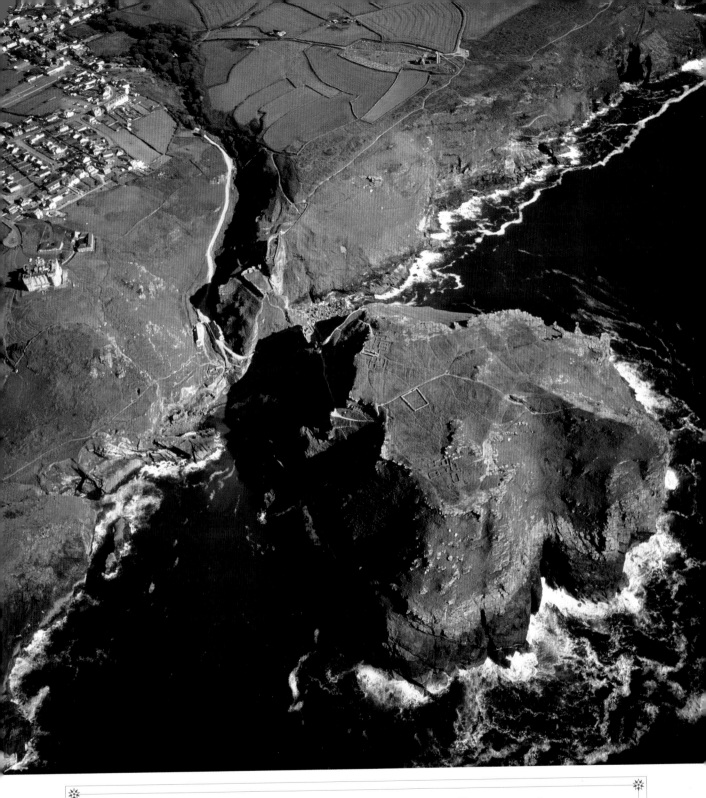

TIN MINES NEAR CAPE CORNWALL (LEFT)

THE GRANITE THAT MAKES UP MUCH OF CORNWALL contains vertical fissures rich in minerals — tin, lead, copper, zinc, iron and silver. The Romans capitalised on it and started a trade that flourished until the 19th century, bringing wealth to coastal villages and ports. The structure of the mineral fissures required a great many deep mines with engine houses to pump out water. Sturdily built, it is these engine houses that survive as ghostly reminders of the past, scattered across the landscape.

TINTAGEL (ABOVE)

LEGEND HAS IT THAT KING ARTHUR was born here in this wild, windswept place on the north coast of Cornwall — a rocky promontory surrounded on three sides by sea and precipitous dark cliffs. There are many ruins here. A Celtic monastery was built around AD500 but abandoned after the Norman conquest. King Arthur's castle was built here in 1145 by the Normans. Originally attached to the mainland, erosion by the sea has worn away the rock so it is reached by climbing steep steps.

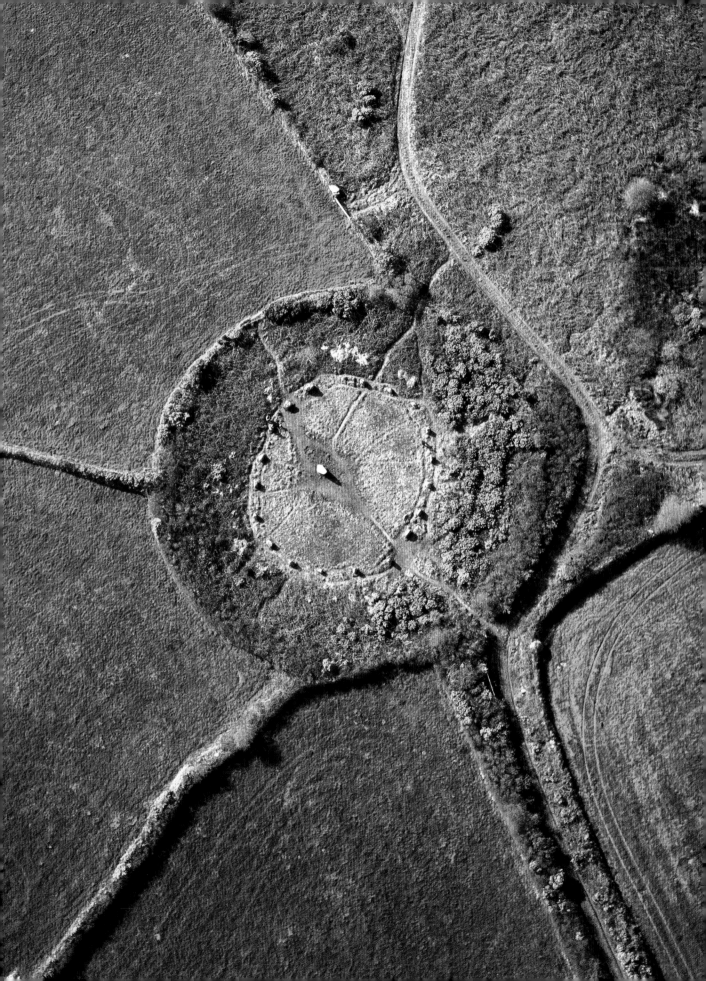

ANCIENT PLACES

ANCIENT COMMUNITIES LEFT MANY SIGNS of their
existence on the British landscape. Hill forts, dwellings,
burial chambers, and roads are the most obvious but
dotted here and there are standing stones. Sometimes a
single stone, sometimes a group, sometimes arranged in
rows, sometimes in circles, they have astronomical
significance and offer clues to the beliefs and practices of
peoples who disappeared long ago.

BOSCAWEN-UN STONE CIRCLE (left)
is situated just to the north of St Buryan and
dates back to around 2000BC.

CHYSAUSTER (above) is a remarkably well-preserved
Iron Age village some 3km (2 miles) north of Trevarrack,
believed to have still been in use during the Roman
occupation. It is an example of a courtyard village,
consisting of nine oval stone-built houses, many of them
built in pairs. Each house has a stone-paved courtyard
with a circular living room and smaller rooms off it, which
may have been used for storing food or keeping animals.
The inhabitants made a living by extracting tin from a
nearby river and taking it to merchants at
St Michael's Mount.

CASTLE-AN-DINAS (right) is an Iron Age hill fort with
triple ramparts, only 1km (half a mile) north-west of
Chysauster, which may have had some strategic
connection with the village. Roger's Tower, on the
southern side of the castle, is a folly built around 1800.

CHINA CLAY QUARRIES (ABOVE)

ST AUSTELL IS THE CHINA CLAY CAPITAL of Cornwall. Nearby, great white spoil heaps from the quarries rise like mountains. No wonder they have become known as the Cornish Alps. The china clay, used for the manufacture of countless products from paper to porcelain, and from face cream to paint, as well as some medicines, was discovered here in 1755. It is now one of Britain's major exports and the most important site for its production outside China.

MINACK THEATRE (ABOVE)

"MINACK", IN CORNISH, means "rocky place". Hewn from granite slabs, this wonderful open air theatre is perched on high cliffs overlooking the sea. It is the nearest thing to an ancient Greek theatre, and was the inspiration of Rowena Cade (1893-1983). The first play to be staged here was Shakespeare's *The Tempest* in the summer of 1932. Since then Minack has grown in popularity and now enjoys a worldwide reputation.

LIZARD PENINSULA (LEFT)

THE LIZARD PENINSULA encompasses the southernmost point of England which is not Lizard Point itself but is located much nearer the lighthouse by Polbream Cove. The lighthouse was built in 1753 to keep ships clear of the majestic cliffs and treacherous rocks that extend out from the shore. The name "Lizard" derives from the Cornish word "Lis-Arth" meaning "Holy Palace".

EDEN PROJECT (ABOVE)

THE LARGEST BOTANICAL GARDEN IN THE WORLD opened in March
2001. Dominating the site are the huge biomes: the humid tropics biome,
for example, at over 200m long and up to 50m high, is one of the largest
greenhouses in the world. It is maintained at a constant 30°C and at high
humidity. It contains tens of thousands of plants and trees from the lush
rainforests of South America, west Africa, Tropical Islands and Asia. It is a
truly ambitious and constantly evolving project.

ST MICHAEL'S MOUNT
(ABOVE AND BACK COVER)

A FEW HUNDRED METRES OFFSHORE FROM **MARAZION** in Cornwall, St. Michael's Mount rises high out of the water. At some time in its history the island may have been permanently connected to the mainland, but now it is only possible to walk across to the island on a causeway at low tide. A Benedictine monastery was founded here in 1044 by the monks of Mont Saint Michel off the coast of Brittany to which it bears a close resemblance. Its potential as a fortress was soon recognised however, and in 1425 the Crown took control of it. In 1657, it was bought by the St Aubyn family then, in 1954, the National Trust acquired it for the nation.

TRURO (RIGHT)

TRURO IS CORNWALL'S ONLY CITY, although Bodmin is the capital of the county. Truro Cathedral was completed in 1910, built in the heart of the old part of the city on the site of the parish church of St Mary. Many of the materials used, from granite to copper, were Cornish in origin. In the Middle Ages, Truro was an important port for the export of mineral ore. In the 18th century it became a fashionable place to live and, as a result, has some fine Georgian houses.

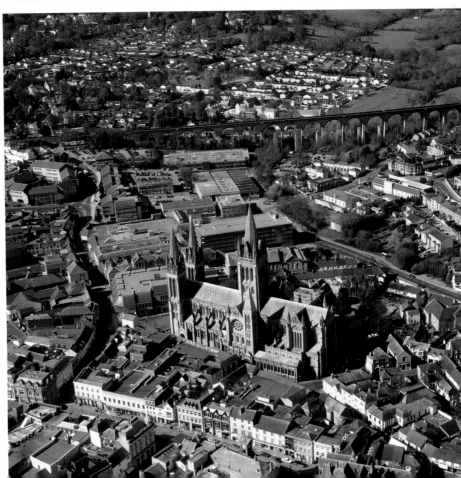

RESTORMEL CASTLE (LEFT)

BUILT IN THE 11TH CENTURY, RESTORMEL CASTLE, near Lostwithiel in Cornwall, is a fine example of a medieval shell keep. By the 13th century it became the property of the Duchy of Cornwall and, as such, belonged to Edward III's son, the Black Prince (1330-1376). In 1644 at the battle of Lostwithiel the castle was captured by Richard Grenville for the King. Sadly, centuries of neglect have taken their toll although a walk through the ruin gives an insight into how it might have looked in its heyday.

PENZANCE (RIGHT)

PENZANCE IS CORNWALL'S OLDEST coastal resort town. Penzance owes its origin to the tin trade and, perhaps, to smuggling. In 1595 the Spaniards burned the town but it was rebuilt quickly only to be ravaged during the Civil War. Penzance was the birthplace of Sir Humphry Davy, the world famous inventor of the miner's safety lamp. Today it is a busy port and starting point for trips to the Scilly Isles.

ST IVES (LEFT)

ST IVES, on the northern side of the Cornish peninsula, is a very picturesque town and is extremely popular with artists. In the 19th century it was a successful pilchard fishing port, and today it is a haven for tourists who come to enjoy the atmosphere of its harbour, its steep narrow streets and alleys, and the surfing beach at Porthmoor.

SCILLY ISLES

THE SCILLY ISLES ARE ONLY 40KM (25 miles) from Land's End but here is a different world, a charming archipelago of 150 islands and islets with clear waters, white sandy beaches and quaint villages. It is a curious fact that more people lived on the islands in ancient times than do now. Of 250 Bronze Age tombs known in England and Wales, 50 are in the Scillies. For centuries smuggling was the main source of income for the peoples of Scilly but now the economy relies largely on the export of flowers and tourism. **TRESCO** (above) is generally considered to be the most beautiful of the islands. The Abbey gardens contain exotic and tropical plants from all over the world.
ST MARY'S (right) is the largest of the islands. The main airport is here as is Hugh Town, with its 18th and 19th century granite buildings.

TAMAR (RIGHT)

TWO BRIDGES SPAN THE **T**AMAR **ESTUARY**, linking Plymouth in Devon with Saltash in Cornwall. A marvel in construction, Brunel's famous Royal Albert railway bridge, completed in 1859, now runs in parallel with a road suspension bridge opened in 1961, at the time the longest suspension bridge in Britain. The river Tamar rises close to the north coast and flows southwards for 80km forming the boundary between Devon and Cornwall. The Tamar valley is an area of outstanding beauty.

TORQUAY (BELOW)

DURING THE **N**APOLEONIC WARS, the British fleet anchored off Torquay to protect England from invasion. At that time it was just a fishing village, but during the 19th century, with the arrival of the railway, it grew rapidly to become a renowned resort. With its palm trees, stylish houses and moored yachts, Torquay evokes a riviera atmosphere and is one of the most popular west country holiday and retirement destinations.

DAWLISH WARREN AND EXMOUTH (ABOVE)

ORIGINALLY, DAWLISH WARREN consisted of two parallel sand spits. A stretch of sand dunes covered by marram grass, it offers solitude even in summer amid a sea of yellow lupin and views of Exmouth, in Devon. Exmouth, at the mouth of the river Exe, was a fishing village that grew into a ferry port in the 13th century. Later, Sir Walter Raleigh sailed on many of his voyages from here. When the railway arrived in 1861, it boomed as a holiday resort town.

CASTLE DROGO (LEFT)

ON THE EDGE OF DARTMOOR, a vast high moorland, Castle Drogo was designed in 1910 by Sir Edwin Lutyens for Sir Julius Drewe. It stands on a hilltop site near the village of Drewsteignton and overlooks the spectacular Devon valley of the river Teign. Sir Julius had discovered that a Norman baron, Drogo de Teigne, was his ancestor and was determined to build a castle on the land that once belonged to him. It was painstakingly constructed from granite blocks over twenty years and the interior is Medieval in style with long passageways and a grand staircase.

EXETER CATHEDRAL (RIGHT)

ONE OF BRITAIN'S OLDEST CITIES, Exeter is the administrative capital of Devon. It was founded by the Romans who built a great red stone wall around it, part of which can still be seen today. A cathedral was constructed in 1050, and then rebuilt by the Normans. In the 13th century it was demolished except for the two towers which were incorporated into the present magnificent building. Although German bombs flattened most of Exeter in May 1942, the cathedral miraculously survived.

LUNDY ISLAND (PREVIOUS PAGE)

LUNDY IS SITUATED OFF THE COAST OF NORTH DEVON in the Bristol Channel. A granite outcrop not quite 6km (3.5 miles) long, its western side is braced against the powerful Atlantic swell, with nothing between it and America. With tales of Vikings, pirates and intrigue, the history of Lundy stretches back to Neolithic times. Today there are only a few permanent residents who enjoy island life, which is peaceful and unspoilt. Lundy's flora and fauna is rich and diverse. Most of the island is a Site of Special Interest and many visitors come to watch birds.

SOUTH DEVON COAST

BETWEEN BEER AND BRANSCOMBE is **BEER HEAD** (below), the most westerly white chalk cliff in England. It reaches a height of 130m and has caves that have been used by smugglers. The white chalk has been quarried locally since Roman times, providing the striking white pillars for many Devon churches and for Exeter Cathedral. A few kilometres further west, near Budleigh Salterton, the rock changes dramatically. At **LADRAM BAY** (right), red Permian sandstone crags rise from the sea with evocative names such as the Tower of Babel, the Razor and the Lost World.

LYNTON AND LYNMOUTH
(ABOVE)

LYNMOUTH IS SITUATED where
the river Lyn meets the sea; Lynton is
perched almost vertically above it,
some 165m above the sea. The north
Devon scenery here is spectacular
with steep ravines, tumbling and
cascading river waters and high cliffs.
In the Middle Ages Lynmouth was a
prosperous herring fishing village
although somewhat cut off from the
rest of the world. The railway, then
roads, started to bring visitors who
were attracted by its savage beauty.
One night in 1952, after severe rains,
the river flooded in a deluge that
destroyed Lynmouth, sweeping
boulders, trees, houses, cars and
people out into the sea.
Many lives were lost.

TAW AND TORRIDGE ESTUARY (LEFT)

THE MOST IMPORTANT DEVON RIVERS flowing into the Bristol Channel, the Taw and the Torridge meet in a common estuary. The river Taw rises on Dartmoor and flows northwards across Devon pastures and finally through the town of Barnstaple. The river Torridge rises far away in Cornwall near the source of the river Tamar, and flows in a wide circuitous route towards Bideford and Appledore where it meets the Taw.

MORTE POINT AND THE NORTH DEVON COAST (ABOVE)

MORTE POINT JUTS OUT INTO THE ATLANTIC from the north Devon coast. Between here and distant Somerset are sheer cliffs up to 300m high. It is a dramatic coastline under constant attack by the powerful Atlantic surf. Small rivers running off Exmoor cut narrow ravines in the cliffs and form plunging waterfalls. There are few villages along this remote, wild and precipitous coast but rocky ledges provide refuges for seabirds.

CAPSTONE POINT, ILFRACOMBE
(ABOVE)

ILFRACOMBE IS THE ONLY SEAPORT for large ships on the whole north Devon coast. Its harbour was important throughout the Middle Ages. In the 19th century steamers from here ran regular services to Bristol, South Wales, Ireland and France. The arrival of the railway led to a decline in shipping but tourists began to come, attracted by Ilfracombe's exceptionally beautiful setting, charming natural harbour and elegant Victorian architecture.

DARTMOOR PRISON (LEFT)

THE WORLD FAMOUS PRISON, at Princetown, Devon, was built in 1806 to house French prisoners from the Napoleonic Wars. Between 1812 and 1816 about 1,500 American and French prisoners died in the prison and were buried in a field beyond the prison walls. Some had been brutally mistreated. Unoccupied for over 30 years, Dartmoor was reopened in 1850 as a civilian prison for convicts sentenced to long terms of imprisonment.

DUNKERY BEACON (ABOVE)

THE HIGHEST POINT IN THE NATIONAL PARK of Exmoor rises to 520m. The summit is the site of an ancient warning network, hence the name beacon, where fires were lit to celebrate national events or to warn of possible invasion. Exmoor is renowned for its beauty. Fringed by the north Devon coast with cliffs up to 300m high, Exmoor has wild moorland, ancient forest, valleys, and a rolling patchwork of fields.

DUNSTER CASTLE (RIGHT)

ON THE EDGE OF EXMOOR,
Dunster Castle dominates a steep
hill overlooking the picturesque
village of Dunster. The Castle has
only changed hands twice since the
Norman conquest of 1066 – the
Mohuns until 1376 and the Luttrells
from then until 1976 when it was
taken over by the National Trust and
opened to the public. Nothing now
remains of the early buildings but the
13th century gatehouse. The present
buildings are of the 17th to 19th
century. During the early medieval
period the sea reached the base of
the hill offering a natural defence, but
the sea has slowly receded and it is
now several miles away.

BRISTOL (LEFT)

BRISTOL IS THE LARGEST CITY in the south-west of England. It is an important cultural centre with a thriving university community. It grew in Saxon times at the confluence of the rivers Avon and Frome when a bridge was built there and the settlement was called Brigstow. The famous **CLIFTON SUSPENSION BRIDGE** (pictured left) was designed by Isambard Kingdom Brunel, who was also responsible for the Great Western Railway and the SS Great Britain. The suspension bridge, with a span of 214m at a height of 75m above the Avon, was opened in December 1864. Originally intended only for horse-drawn carriages, the bridge now carries 4 million cars each year.

BATH (ABOVE)

NEARLY TWO THOUSAND YEARS AGO, the Romans built their spa of Aquae Sulis around Britain's only hot mineral springs at Bath. The waters are thought to originate from rainwater which fell on the Mendip Hills to the south over 20,000 years ago. They rise from a depth of about 3000m at a constant temperature of 46.5°C. For centuries the healing properties of the hot mineral water have attracted visitors, and led to a unique historic urban environment around the springs. The central area of Bath, now a World Heritage City, is a planned town of Georgian architecture built with liberal use of mellow coloured Bath stone.

GLASTONBURY FESTIVAL
(RIGHT)

IN 1970 MICHAEL EAVIS, of Pilton, decided to stage a music festival on his farm. Today, the Glastonbury Festival is the UK's biggest outdoor pop festival and one of the most famous regular rock festivals in the world attracting well over 100,000 visitors and raising money for charities.

WELLS CATHEDRAL
(BELOW)

WITH A POPULATION OF only about 10,000, Wells in Somerset is the smallest city in England but its cathedral, of which construction began in 1180, is an architectural delight, with a unique scissors arch to support the central tower. The Bishop's Palace, moated home of the Bishop of Bath and Wells, and Vicars Close, a charming 14th-century street joined to the cathedral are among the fine medieval buildings that survive in Wells.

GLASTONBURY TOR (ABOVE)

LEGEND HAS IT THAT JOSEPH OF ARIMATHEA buried the chalice used at the Last Supper at the spring that rises on the slopes of the Tor, a prominent and striking natural hill that rises from the Somerset levels. Excavations have suggested occupation of the hill as far back as the 6th century. A monastery of St Michael existed here early in the medieval period, and terracing on the slopes of the Tor indicates strip lynchets for cultivation from that time. The monastery probably came under the control of Glastonbury Abbey. An earthquake destroyed the church in 1275 but it was rebuilt in the 14th century. At the time of the dissolution of Glastonbury Abbey in 1539, the last abbott and two of his monks were hanged on the Tor. The church became a ruin but the tower was restored in the 18th century. The Tor is in the care of the National Trust.

NETHER STOWEY CASTLE (RIGHT)

AN EARLY NORMAN MOTTE CASTLE was built in the 12th century on the northern fringe of the Quantocks in Somerset by William Fitzodo. It was abandoned in 1485. Not much is left except for the wall foundations of the stone keep which are still visible.

MUCHELNEY (LEFT)

IN A QUAINT VILLAGE on the Somerset Levels are the ruins of a Benedictine monastery, established around AD950. All that exists of the abbey church today are a few foundation walls, but evidence suggests that it was a rather magnificent building. During its history it had been raided by Vikings but survived and indeed flourished until its dissolution in 1532. Then its great abbey church was systematically destroyed and sold for building stone but the abbot's house still stands.

BRENT KNOLL (RIGHT)

AN IRON AGE FORT is located on an isolated hill not far from Burnham-on-Sea. This site was later used by both Romans and the Anglo-Saxons as a refuge against raiding Danes. The interior of the fort has been damaged by quarrying for Lias limestone which caps the hill, and trenches on the northern side were used by military personnel during the Second World War.

SOMERSET LEVELS

THE LEVELS, ONCE INUNDATED BY THE SEA, gradually became a vast area of salt marsh. Prone to **FLOODING** (above), rivers were diverted by settlers, and now a complex network of channels helps drain the land. Frequently swathed in **LOW LYING MIST** (right) that adds a touch of mystery and magic to this place, the Levels are bounded by the uplands of the Mendips, the Quantocks and the Brendon Hills. As long as 6,000 years ago, people built wooden trackways across the marshes to provide access to settlements and hunting areas. At Sedgemoor, in 1685, the last battle to be fought on English soil took place when the Protestant rebellion led by the Duke of Monmouth was defeated by the army of King James II.

LAST REFUGE Ltd

Nature is a precious inheritance, to be cared for and cherished by all of us. Last Refuge Ltd is a small company primarily dedicated to documenting and archiving endangered environments and species in our rapidly changing world, through films, images and research. The company was established in 1992 for a study of wild giant pandas in the Qinling mountains of central China, which seemed, literally, to be the "last refuge" for these charismatic animals. The company continued to embrace new projects worldwide. Two films on lemurs in Madagascar quickly followed and the ring-tailed lemur became the company's logo. Adrian Warren and Dae Sasitorn, who run the company from a farmhouse in Somerset, have created a special website, www.lastrefuge.co.uk, in order to present their work. This is becoming a huge resource for information, and an extensive photographic archive of still and moving images for both education and media. Ultimately they hope to offer special conservation awards to fund work by others.

ADRIAN WARREN

Adrian Warren is a biologist and a commercial pilot, with over 30 years' experience as a photographer and filmmaker. He has worked worldwide for the BBC Natural History Unit, and as a director in the IMAX giant screen format. He has recently designed a new wing-mounted camera system for aircraft to further develop his interest in aviation, aerial filming and photography. As a stills photographer, he has a personal photographic archive of over 100,000 pictures, with worldwide coverage of wildlife, landscapes, aerials, and peoples. His photographs appear in books, magazines, advertisements, posters, calendars, greetings cards and many other products. His awards include a Winston Churchill Fellowship; the Cherry Kearton Medal from the Royal Geographical Society in London; the Genesis award from the Ark Trust for Conservation; an International Prime Time Emmy; and the Golden Eagle Award from New York.

DAE SASITORN

Dae Sasitorn is an academic from the world of chemistry but has given it up to follow her love for the natural world. She manages the company and is a computer expert. She has created, designed and manages the Last Refuge website as well as scanning thousands of images for the archive. She is also a first-class photographer in her own right.

THE PHOTOGRAPHY

Adrian and Dae operate their own Cessna 182G out of a tiny farm strip close to their house. They bought the single engined four-seater aircraft in May 1999 in order to develop a new wing-mounted camera system for cinematography. The 1964 Cessna was in beautiful condition, and had only one previous owner. It is the perfect aircraft for aerial work: small, manoeuvrable, with plenty of power, and the high wing configuration offering an almost unrestricted view on the world below. With 20 degrees of flap it is possible to fly as slowly as 60 knots. The cabin side window opens upwards and outwards and is kept open by the airflow. The photographs were taken on Hasselblad medium format 6 x 6 cm cameras and lenses using Fujichrome Velvia film. Waiting for the right weather, with a clear atmosphere and less than 50 per cent cloud cover, required being on standby for months.

First Published in 2009 by Myriad Books Limited,
35 Bishopsthorpe Road, London, SE26

Photographs and Text ©
Dae Sasitorn and Adrian Warren
Last Refuge Limited

ISBN 1 84746 227 8
EAN 978 1 184746 227 5

Designed by Dae Sasitorn and Adrian Warren
Last Refuge Limited
Printed in China